CLUB 7

7 HEAVEN
The Official Book

Jordan Paramor

PUFFIN BOOKS

PUFFIN BOOKS

Published by the Penguin Group
Penguin Books Ltd, 80 Strand, London WC2R 0RL, England
Penguin Putnam Inc., 375 Hudson Street, New York, New York 10014, USA
Penguin Books Australia Ltd, Ringwood, Victoria, Australia
Penguin Books Canada Ltd, 10 Alcorn Avenue, Toronto, Ontario, Canada M4V 3B2
Penguin Books India (P) Ltd, 11 Community Centre, Panchsheel Park, New Delhi – 110 017, India
Penguin Books (NZ) Ltd, Cnr Rosedale and Airborne Roads, Albany, Auckland, New Zealand
Penguin Books (South Africa) (Pty) Ltd, 24 Sturdee Avenue, Rosebank 2196, South Africa

Penguin Books Ltd, Registered Offices: 80 Strand, London WC2R 0RL, England

www.penguin.com

First published 2001
1

Written by Jordan Paramor

Photography by Julian Barton
Additional Photography by Michael Segal, Shonadh French & Charlotte Martin
Backstage photography, pages 24-27 © 2001 Julian Barton, supplied courtesy of Idols Licensing & Publicity Ltd

Printed and bound in Great Britain by Butler & Tanner

British Library Cataloguing in Publication Data
A CIP catalogue record for this book is available from the British Library

ISBN 0–141–31460–5

A massive hello and welcome to our brand-new book. If you fancy discovering the secrets of our new TV series, getting all the backstage gossip from our S Club Party 2001 tour and finding out

how we all got where we are today, then you've come to the right place. And that's not all. If you're desperate to get the inside track on our new single and album, and the exclusive gossip on our forthcoming film, it's all inside. We've had the most incredible time being in S Club 7 for the past three years, and we really hope you've all enjoyed being a part of it too. Thank you for being the most fantastic fans a band could have and get ready, because there's plenty more to come.

Well, what are you waiting for? Dive on in!

Love Tina xxx

Hannah xxx

Rachel x

CLUB 7

That Thing You Bring

Each member of S Club 7 brings their own special something to the band. Here, their fellow band mates spill the beans on just what that is ...

"The most obvious thing Jo brings to the band is her incredibly rich voice. She sings a lot of the leads because her voice is very, very, very good and really strong. I think Jo also gives the band a feisty edge because even though she's girlie, she's cool and powerful."
Tina

"Paul is very funny and he's got a lot of character. He can be quite changeable, and one minute he's really loud and the next he can be quite quiet. He's a bit of a thinker. But I think he brings a lot of humour to the band because he's really animated and comical."
Rachel

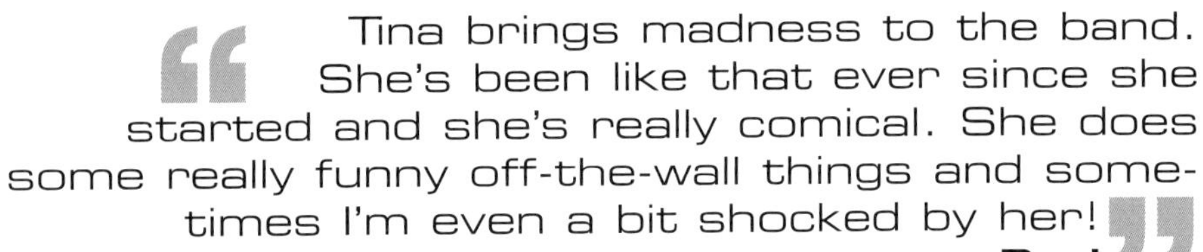

"Tina brings madness to the band. She's been like that ever since she started and she's really comical. She does some really funny off-the-wall things and sometimes I'm even a bit shocked by her!"
Paul

"Jon brings humour to the band. He helps us through some of the days that can be a bit long. He also keeps his calm under pressure. When things get tedious he makes everyone laugh at the right time and brings light to the day when we're all a bit tired."
Hannah

"Bradley's a great songwriter, producer and a fantastic singer, so he brings all of those skills. And he's great to watch on stage too. He's a real all-rounder."
Jo

"I always watch what everyone's doing when we're performing on-stage and Hannah's definitely always feeling the vibe. I think there are a lot of girls out there who want to be Hannah's mate because she looks like she'd be cool and a laugh, and they're right."
Bradley

"Rachel brings glamour to the band. She and Jo have countless conversations about hair, clothes and everything. Together they're the girlie element!"
Jon

Growing Up the S CLUB Way

They've travelled the world, won countless awards and had numerous chart-topping hits, but have you ever wondered how S Club 7 came to become the top pop stars they are today? All is revealed as we take a peek into their early years, chart their rise to fame and discover how their dreams really did come true ...

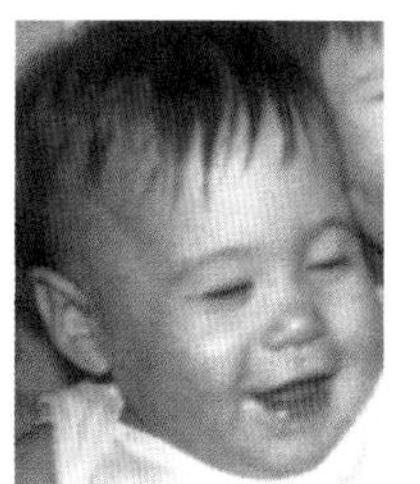
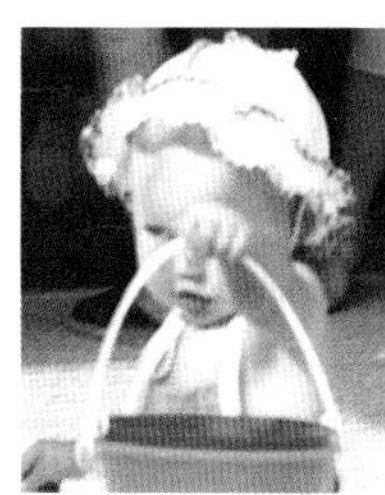

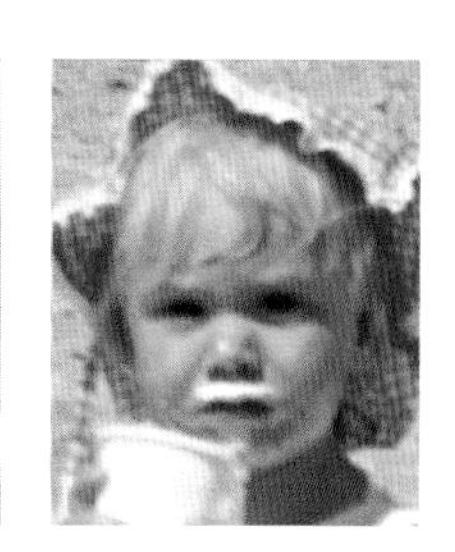

'What I remember most about growing up is how tight we were as a family.'

Rachel casts her mind back to her early years. 'We all used to go out together a lot, to the seaside and stuff. I remember being about four and being stung on my backside by a wasp! I think that's my earliest memory. I also remember being on the rides at the seaside when I was about six or seven. We had a lot of fun together as a family.'

North-London lass Rachel was very girlie when she was young, and aged seven she got into the habit of trying on her mum's dresses and make-up. Perhaps preparing for her later glamorous S Club days?

'Probably!' she laughs. 'I loved make-up and being really feminine. I started ballet classes when I was about five and even then I think I knew I wanted to be in the entertainment business. But I also used to go out riding my bike with the other kids up my road, so I had that side to me as well.'

Rachel has fond memories of school but she readily admits that she was more interested in hanging out with her friends than doing her homework.

'I wasn't really academic. I was more creative, and preferred classes like drama and art. I guess I was kind of an average student. I wasn't particularly naughty, but I was a bit cheeky. If I was told not to wear jewellery to school I would, and I would always customize my clothes to make my uniform look a bit different.'

Needless to say, Rachel was always in demand with the guys. She remembers having her first kiss during a game of Spin the Bottle round at a friend's house. 'We were in a cupboard for some strange reason. It was very odd. At least I won't forget it in a hurry!'

Rachel's first taste of fame came aged twelve when she won a modelling competition in *J-17* magazine.

'My mum saw the competition and said that I should enter it for a laugh, so I did. Then a month afterwards I got a letter through the post saying that I'd won. I got picked up by a limousine and had my hair and make-up done

'We had a lot of fun together as a family.'

'I was a bit cheeky.'

and everything. It was fantastic. I did some other bits and pieces of modelling afterwards for hair magazines and things, but nothing serious.'

From the age of fifteen, Rachel worked in a local shoe shop on Saturdays.

'I absolutely loved working there. It was a real laugh and they sold wicked shoes. I used to come home with a nice new pair practically every Saturday.'

After leaving school, Rachel attended The London College of Fashion for two years where she did a GNVQ in business fashion. Once she graduated, she landed a job with a film company before going to work for a fashion-PR company. It was during this time that she was spotted and asked to try out for S Club 7, as she explains: 'My brother works for a record company and I went to meet him for lunch one day, and there happened to be a couple of record producers in his canteen. They asked me if I could sing and if I would go into a studio and record a song, which I did. Our manager Simon Fuller heard the tape and liked it. So we met up and the rest is history!'

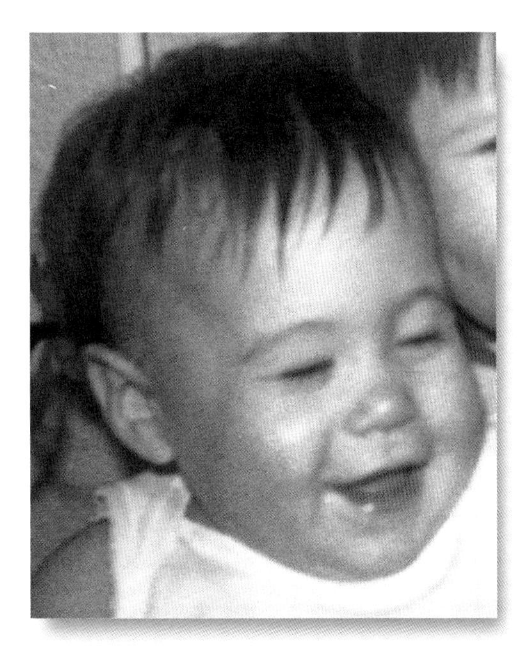

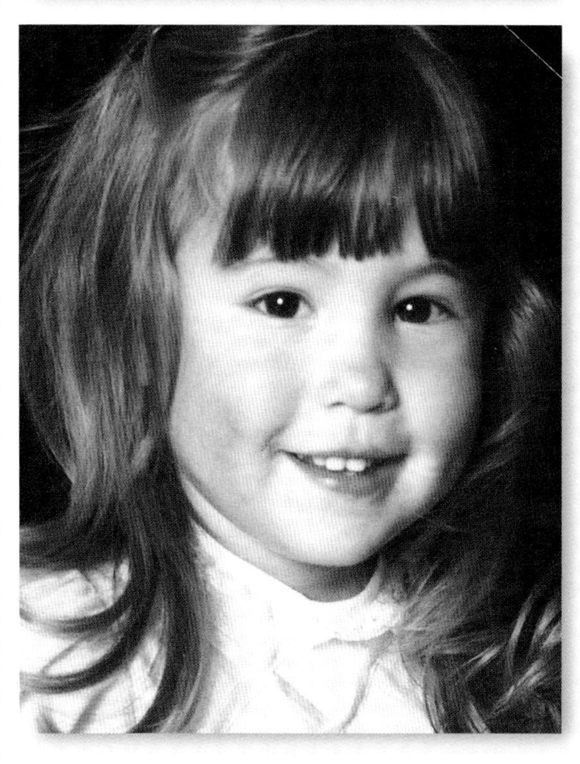

From top left, clockwise: Rachel aged one, fourteen, three and five years.

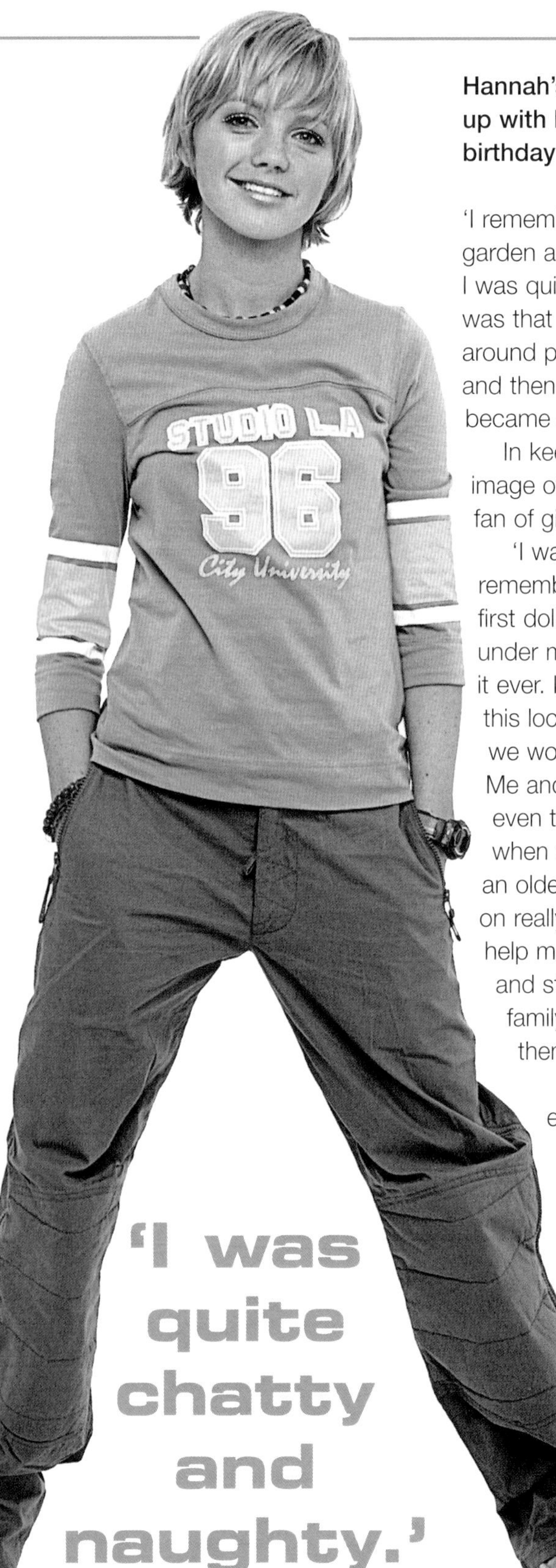

'I was quite chatty and naughty.'

Hannah's earliest memory of growing up with her family in Norfolk is her birthday party, aged three.

'I remember playing games in the garden and having a wicked time. I think I was quite chatty and naughty when I was that age. I really enjoyed being around people when I was a toddler, and then when I hit about seven I became a bit shyer.'

In keeping with her cute tomboy image of today, Hannah wasn't a big fan of girlie toys as a child.

'I was really into Meccano, and I remember when my mum bought my first doll I kicked up such a fuss. I put it under my bed and refused to play with it ever. I was much happier playing in this local field with my brother, where we would climb trees and build dens. Me and my brother were really close, even though we used to fight a lot when we were growing up. I've got an older sister, Tanya, as well. We got on really well and she always used to help me out with my dancing classes and stuff. We were a really happy family and I get on even better with them all nowadays.'

School days were pretty enjoyable for Hannah, who was cheeky, but managed to get away with quite a lot by flashing her sweet smile at the teachers. That same smile also worked with the boys. However, when it came to her first boyfriend, it seems that Hannah's motto was, 'Share and share alike'.

'In junior school, me and two of my friends all decided to go out with the same boy at the same time. I don't know how we worked that one out, but looking back it seemed to work out quite well,' she says, smiling.

Needless to say, Hannah was a big fan of music lessons throughout her school days.

'I really enjoyed PE, and I was also a fan of maths and science classes. But music was always my favourite subject.'

Secondary school was a busy time for Hannah, who had loads of hobbies outside school and would regularly attend dance classes and compete in swimming galas. When she was thirteen she landed a place in the National Youth Music Theatre, after spotting an audition in *The Stage* showbiz newspaper. It was there that she met a certain young man called Paul Cattermole.

'The National Youth Music Theatre was a company that would put on productions in the school holidays, so I would go and stay in youth hostels in London while we rehearsed. Paul used to go as well and I met him because my mate, Sheridan, fancied him, and I fancied his best mate, Neil. I think Paul thought me and my friend were a bit giggly because we used to follow him and Neil around.'

The theatre group provided Hannah with some brilliant performing experience and, after several TV appearances, Hannah heard about the auditions for S Club 7 and decided to 'go along for a laugh'.

'I never expected anything to come of the audition and couldn't believe it when I got in,' says Hannah. 'The whole S Club experience has been so brilliant and so hectic. It's been really fun sometimes, and really tiring at other times. But we always manage to have a laugh whatever and I absolutely love it.'

'Music was always my favourite subject.'

From top left, clockwise: Hannah aged fifteen, one, three and six years.

hannah

Looking at him now, it's hard to believe that Paul was a quiet chap when he was young.

'I was really quiet actually, but I was also full of energy and quite a handful for my mum at times,' he says. 'I was quite boisterous and I could be a bit stroppy sometimes. I can remember my young days quite well and my earliest memory is being bathed in the sink at my house when I was about two.'

Paul describes his school days as 'all right,' and says that although he got into his fair share of trouble, he would often get himself out of it again by giving the teacher a cheeky wink.

'I would make a joke and the teachers would think it was funny, so a lot of the time they'd let me off. But I was never terrible. I never hung around with a really bad crowd or got into fights or anything. In secondary school my favourite subjects were English, maths and science, and I planned on being a racing-car driver or a physicist. But I changed my mind all the time.'

Due to his shyness, Paul admits that he didn't have much luck with the ladies in his early years.

'I didn't really have many girlfriends back then because I think I've always been a bit shy. Even now I am. People take me for incredibly confident because I'm loud, but loud people aren't always the most confident ones.'

While still at school, Paul auditioned and won a part in the National Youth Music Theatre (where he remembers only too clearly a young Hannah pursuing his mate Neil!) and he gained valuable experience in several productions.

After leaving school, he went on to do a BTEC in Performing Arts at Barnet College, alongside none other than Spice Girl Emma Bunton.

'We didn't know each other that well, although we did sing a duet together once. We still stop and chat when we see each other around now, but half the time we're rushing about so we just about have time to say a quick hello.'

Paul then went to a musical theatre school, where he did a course which set him up well for the future. 'I learned more in those three years than I'd ever learned anywhere else. It was a

'I think I've always been a bit shy.'

paul

brilliant experience.'

During this time he formed his first rock band, and says of it, 'I had an amazing time doing that. The gigs we played were small, but I loved every second of it.'

But fate stepped in and lured him away to the world of pop when he was spotted by some talent scouts employed by S Club 7's manager, Simon Fuller.

'They came to my college and saw me perform. I was asked to audition for the band and I got in – it's as simple as that! I'm really pleased that things have worked out the way they did. I'm having such an amazing time being in the band. It's full-on, but it's brilliant.'

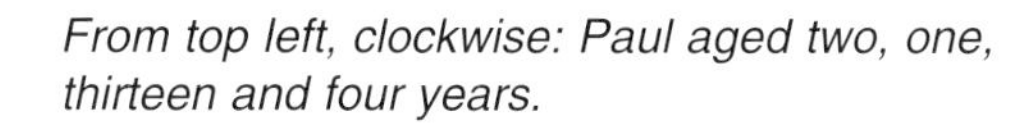

From top left, clockwise: Paul aged two, one, thirteen and four years.

'I planned on being a racing-car driver.'

jon

Jon's earliest memories are dominated by his two dogs, a greyhound called Sheba and a German shepherd called Kelly.

'They were a part of the family before I was born, so they were always around when I was younger,' he says affectionately. 'I remember when I was about three or four, I used to try and run up the stairs and Sheba would run after me and grab the bottom of my trousers and drag me back down again. We always played that game!'

Jon has two older brothers, but spent a lot of time with his younger sister, Cassie, as they were closer in age.

'When I was about five and she was about two we got on like a house on fire. We used to make up little plays and then act them out for my family, but she would always pull out at the last second and refuse to do it.

'We started to argue a bit more as we got older, but we still played together a lot, and when I was about seven or eight we used to make dens in the back garden out of bushes. We used to pretend that they were fortresses!'

Jon's school days were unusual, to say the least. When he was twelve he landed a part in a London production of *Oliver!*, which meant that he had to move away from his family in Devon and live in London. It was then that he first attended the famous Sylvia Young Theatre School, along with the likes of Billie Piper and Scott Robinson from Five.

'I went there for six months and joined fully when I was about thirteen. That was when my family also moved up to London, which I was really pleased about. I absolutely loved Sylvia's because we did normal subjects on a Monday, Tuesday and Wednesday, and then on Thursdays and Fridays we got to dance, sing and act all day. My favourite subjects were English, drama and music, and I think that generally I was pretty well behaved.'

During this time, Jon did a lot of theatre work, radio plays and musicals, and was fifteen when he landed the part of Josh Haye in *Eastenders*.

'It was so weird being on set because everything is exactly the same as you see it on TV. They'd ask me if I knew where the cafe was and I'd be like, "Yeah, I know where everything is. I've been

'I was pretty well behaved.'

watching *Eastenders* all my life." It was really freaky.'

Jon went for the S Club 7 audition after spotting the advert in *The Stage*.

'It sounded really exciting, so I went and queued up with everyone else and luckily I got it.'

So looking back, does he feel like he missed out on any of the normal every-day things that teenagers do, due to his unusual upbringing?

'I didn't really have time to hang out with my mates or anything, but I didn't mind because I was doing what I loved,' he says honestly. 'I think I've been through every emotion possible being in the band. We've laughed a lot and we've cried a lot, but I wouldn't change it for anything.'

'We got to dance, sing and act all day.'

From the top, clockwise: Jon aged two months, six years old (sister Cassie on right), thirteen and two years.

'I always wanted to dance.'

Chatty Tina says that she was outspoken from an early age. In fact, once she learned to talk, there was no stopping her!

'I was a real chatterbox when I was very young, but I wasn't naughty. I was quite cheeky and I had an answer for everything, which probably drove my parents mad. I also had a really bad habit of drawing on walls, and my first memories are of me scribbling on the walls of my house. My poor parents! I did have quiet moments as well when I could be quite shy, but I think they were pretty rare.'

Tina dreamed of fame even as a very young girl. She was determined to follow her dreams, and started going to dance classes at the age of five.

'I was very aware of what I wanted from a very young age and I was really determined. I always wanted to dance and that was what my life revolved around.'

When she was twelve, Tina went to stage school in London to study dancing. But much as she loved being there, there was a side to it that she hated.

'Stage school was very competitive so it was also quite bitchy at times. I made sure that I never got dragged into that because it wasn't what being there was about. I wanted to dance and have fun, so I learned not to get involved with that side of things. But I think being surrounded by that whole scene made me grow up quickly and toughened me up.'

Thankfully, Tina had some good friends who supported her when drama school got her down.

'I've made some brilliant friends over the years, and I've got one particular friend that I've had since childhood and she's amazing. We've gone through everything together and she's always been there for me.'

As for her first boyfriend?

'It was when I was about five. We used to kiss each other and then say we hated each other and that we thought each other was gross, and then kiss again! It was all very sweet and innocent.'

When it came to schoolwork, like many of her fellow band mates, Tina says that she preferred the creative subjects.

'I really liked all the arty stuff at school and don't think I was particularly academic. I liked the subjects that allowed you to use your imagination. For instance, I loved English where you got to write stories, but I hated maths because I didn't enjoy all the facts and figures. I would much rather have been reading *Macbeth*.'

Tina's parents always encouraged her to be independent when she was growing up, so as soon as she was old enough she got herself a Saturday job as a receptionist.

'It was great because I was earning really good money, so I always had money to go out with my friends and I was able to buy some really cool clothes.'

Tina landed her first professional dancing

job when she was eighteen and went on to have glamorous jobs, dancing onstage for the likes of Simply Red, Toni Braxton and Pulp. And Tina soon found herself in a band for real when she was picked to join S Club 7 after trying her luck at the auditions.

'It's hard to sum up what it's been like being in S Club 7. Every day is different. All seven of us have been on this crazy journey and we never know where it's going to take us next. It's mad!'

From top left, clockwise: Tina aged eight months, at fourteen, twelve and almost two years.

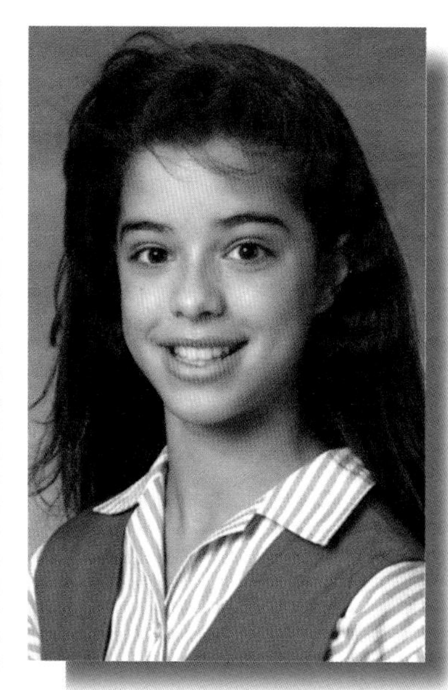

Bradley spent the early years of his life on the road with his parents, who had a successful band called The CoolNotes.

And it'll come as no surprise to hear that the music bug bit him early.

'I remember having my very own drum kit when I was three, which the drummer from my mum and dad's band had specially made for me. The drum sticks had my name on them and everything, and I loved it. I was the happiest little kid in the world.'

Even with his drum kit, Bradley claims that he was quite quiet when he was tiny.

'My mum says that I was really good and I never cried a lot. I was really laid back as a toddler and I still am now. I got on really well with my older sister, Saskia, but I remember always wanting an older brother who would mess around with me and play-fight. Still, me and Saskia used to play-fight and stuff, and I have to say, she was a pretty good fighter!'

School wasn't Bradley's favourite place because he knew from the word go that his heart lay in music.

'I'm not a very good example to other people where school is concerned because I didn't really pay much attention. I didn't realize back then how hard it is to break into the music business, and I know now how incredibly lucky I've been to have got where I am.

'The only subject I really liked at school was graphic design, so I became the class joker in all my other lessons. But I'm not proud of it, and I'm sure things would be different if I went back there now.'

When he reached his mid-teens, Bradley and his schoolmates would regularly hit the town and go to under-eighteens' clubs. And to make sure he always had a bit of cash in his pocket to fund his nights out, he got himself a tele-sales job selling windows and doors.

'Pretty much all my mates worked there as well so it was a really good laugh. It wasn't really like work at all. After I left there I worked at fast-food chains. I always made sure I had a job of some kind.'

There's no doubting that Bradley was a hit with the girls when he was younger, but that didn't stop him having his heart broken at secondary school.

'There was this girl that I really liked for ages and ages and eventually I got to go out with her. But we split after two weeks and I was absolutely gutted. I'd liked her for so long and I couldn't believe it.'

Thankfully, Bradley had his music to take his mind off the split and he formed his first band with his mate Darren while he was still at school.

'We had a Jodeci-type vibe. It was cool. I also had a band with my sister before S Club came along.'

Bradley heard about the S Club 7 auditions through a family friend, but nearly missed out.

'I was in two minds about whether to go, but in the end I decided to go for it. It was my first ever audition and you can imagine how pleased I was when I got in. Even now, when I take a step back and look at everything I think, Wow, it's me! Little Brad from Sutton travelling the world, selling millions of albums, making TV shows and winning a BRIT award. It's just crazy.'

'I was really laid-back as a toddler.'

bradley

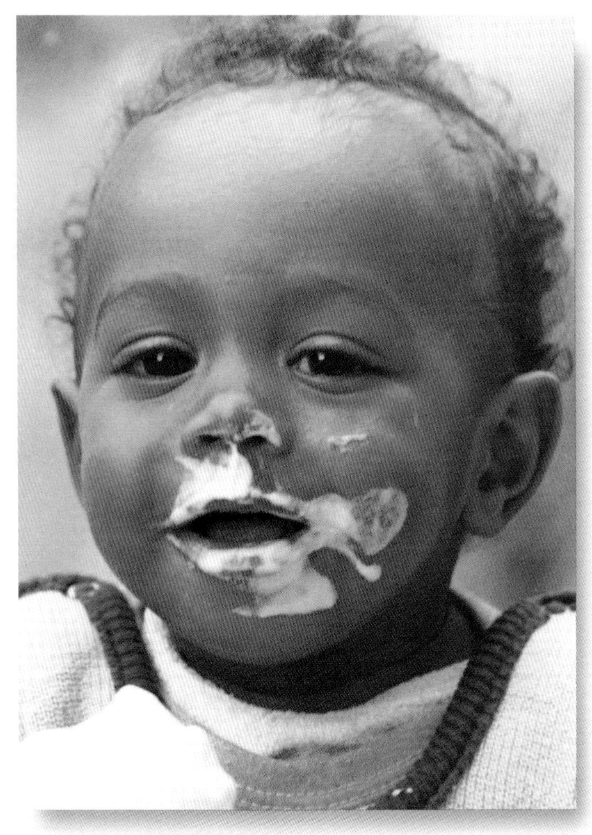

'I became the class joker.'

From top left, clockwise: Bradley aged nine months, eight, fifteen and three years.

jo

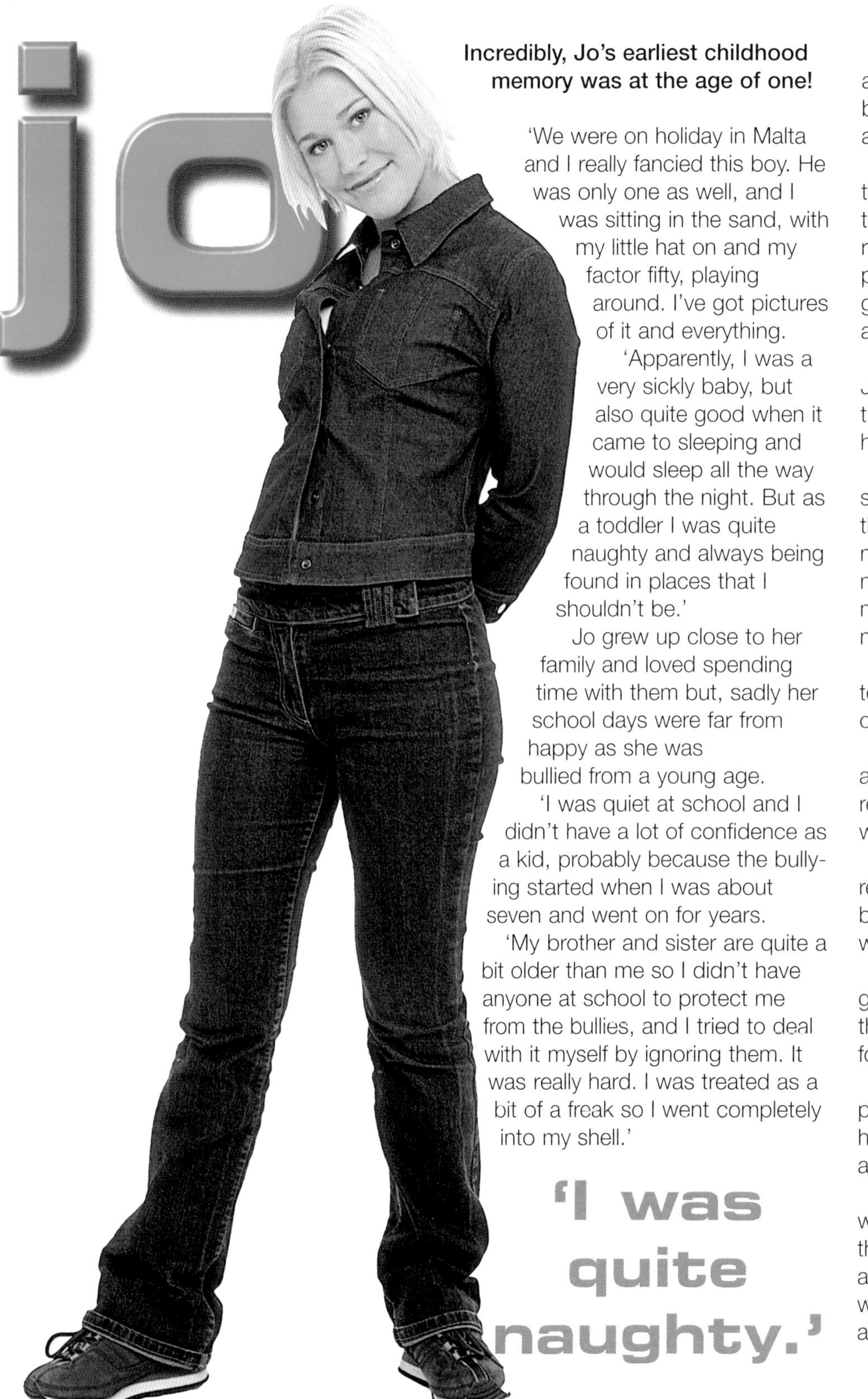

Incredibly, Jo's earliest childhood memory was at the age of one!

'We were on holiday in Malta and I really fancied this boy. He was only one as well, and I was sitting in the sand, with my little hat on and my factor fifty, playing around. I've got pictures of it and everything.

'Apparently, I was a very sickly baby, but also quite good when it came to sleeping and would sleep all the way through the night. But as a toddler I was quite naughty and always being found in places that I shouldn't be.'

Jo grew up close to her family and loved spending time with them but, sadly her school days were far from happy as she was bullied from a young age.

'I was quiet at school and I didn't have a lot of confidence as a kid, probably because the bullying started when I was about seven and went on for years.

'My brother and sister are quite a bit older than me so I didn't have anyone at school to protect me from the bullies, and I tried to deal with it myself by ignoring them. It was really hard. I was treated as a bit of a freak so I went completely into my shell.'

'I was quite naughty.'

Jo was too scared to tell her parents about what was going on at school because the bullies had warned her against it.

'Bullies always tell you not to tell, and they make you think that something terrible will happen if you do. But that's rubbish. When I did eventually tell my parents about what was going on, they got me out of the school straight away and I was so relieved.'

During the hard times, music became Jo's main comfort. Little did she know that it would play such a massive part in her later life.

'I enjoyed quite a lot of my subjects at school, especially history and English, but the school didn't really concentrate on music very heavily, so I would do that in my spare time. It was a huge comfort to me. Somehow just being around music made me feel better.'

Jo had her first boyfriend at the age of ten – a guy called Danny, who she went out with for two years.

'I thought he was the love of my life and I was going to marry him. We got on really well, but then he cheated on me with another girl and broke my heart.'

It was in her early teens that Jo realized that despite initially wanting to become an air hostess, what she really wanted was a career in music.

'Up until then I'd be too shy to even get up on a karaoke machine. But something inside me decided that singing was for me.'

After leaving school, Jo worked in a pet shop and a supermarket before she had her first taste of musical success as a backing singer.

'It was a family friend called Annette who really inspired me to go for it with the singing. She's got the most unbelievable voice and she really helped me out with contacts and stuff. She was amazing.'

Soon Jo found herself working in a

country-and-western theme pub, where she got to sing onstage every night.

'Our hours were six in the evening until midnight, so I got to sleep all day and then sing and have a good time in the evening. It was my perfect job!'

And it was while she was doing the hoedown that she was spotted by someone from S Club 7's management company, 19, who just happened to have popped in for dinner. But it wasn't until two years later that Jo got a phone call from 19 asking her to go along to the S Club 7 auditions.

'I was really nervous going to the auditions because I still wasn't very confident, but I was so, so happy when I got the phone call to say that I'd got into the band. I think at that point, one of the reasons I really wanted to make it as a singer was to show everyone who had given me such a hard time over the years. I know a few of the people who bullied me at school have got kids now, so it gives me real satisfaction to think that those kids are probably going up to them and asking for an S Club 7 CD!

'I've changed so much since being in S Club. I'm really confident and these days I'm doing this for me. The band has given me a whole new lease of life.'

'Just being around music made me feel better.'

From top left, clockwise: Jo aged nine, eight, one and two years.

Let's Hit the Road

Pretend beaches, non-stop parties and missing pants. Welcome to life on tour with S Club 7...

Get Ready to Rock

Doing a huge tour is something that S Club 7 have been dreaming about ever since they first started. Only, they've been in such big demand since becoming pop kings and queens worldwide that it took them a while to find the time to get their S Club Party 2001 tour sorted.

'We were all desperate to get out on the road, but we also wanted to wait until we were totally ready and we could give it our all,' explains Bradley.

'It was something that we would have liked to do a lot earlier on, but things were always so hectic,' adds Hannah. 'I think we all feel like that tour was the best thing we've ever got to do while in S Club 7. We had the time of our lives.'

The band spent weeks rehearsing in a huge house in Bath to make sure that the show was 100% perfect and ready to unleash on their fans. Bring the house down? They certainly did ...

It's Show Time...

S Club 7 performed eighteen songs during their carnival-style musical extravaganza. The equipment and sets for the tour were transported in ten huge lorries, and a crew of 100 people worked on the show every night. Go-karts, balloons, glitter, confetti, a red Cadillac, fireworks and even a parachute were the order of the day. Each night, crowds of over 13,000 fans went wild in the aisles and, despite being a tad nervous in the beginning, the band themselves have nothing but incredible memories.

'I think it would be weird if we hadn't been nervous,' says a smiling Tina, 'but, thankfully, excitement soon took over from the nerves and there was no stopping us. I get a warm feeling every time I look back on the tour.'

Jo and Rachel were so overwhelmed on the first night of the tour that they cried, as Rachel reveals. 'I remember Jo and I being backstage on the first night, and there was a door that you could see the audience through. We had a peek and we got so emotional. We had waited so long for that moment, and to see all the people that had come to see us was such an unbelievable feeling. Jo and I got really soppy, but luckily I managed to stop myself crying onstage.'

Poor Jo wasn't quite so lucky though.

'I cried like a baby onstage,' she laughs. 'We've been together for three years now and we'd never done anything like that before. It was our show. It was so overwhelming to go out onstage and see ten thousand people and know that they were there just to see us. It really hit me that it was real and I couldn't stop crying. My make-up was running down my face and I probably looked a mess, but I didn't care. It was still an amazing moment for me.'

Hannah admits that she also found the first show really nerve-racking, and says, 'I think there was such a build-up to it that the first night was pretty scary. But as time went on, the nerves went and we started letting ourselves go much more.'

Jon and Paul had no problems with first-night nerves, although playing Wembley was a different story for Jon.

'I was fine the first night because as soon as I got out on to the stage I got an adrenalin rush and there's no other feeling like it. But I must admit that I got nervous when we performed at Wembley because I knew that my parents would be watching. That was very scary.'

Bradley says he felt just about every emotion it's possible to feel before going on stage on the opening night.

'I was backstage and I felt excited and nervous and happy and emotional. Actually, I didn't really know how I felt because it was so, so weird. I can't really explain it. But once I got onstage all I felt was incredible. As soon as I get onstage I'm a different person, I go mad. And I really did that night.'

Get on the Bus

When it came to travelling from venue to venue, the guys and girls would while away the hours watching videos and listening to music on their luxury tour bus, which boasted its own kitchen and living-room area.

'I loved being on the tour bus because it's something I've always wanted to do,' says Paul. 'Touring is really what I joined the band for, so I thought it was wicked travelling around and everything.'

Bands often describe a real 'family feel' when they're touring, and it's obvious that the S Club experience was no different. All the dancers and crew became great mates and would hang out together in their spare time. In fact, Bradley would often hop aboard the dancers' bus for a change of scene.

'It was nice to have a whole load of new people around, and I think it helped because we didn't feel like us seven had to be together all of the time. And whereas on our bus we would kind of chill out and take time out, on the dancers' bus they'd have the stereo pumped up and everyone would be up, rapping and dancing. It was wicked.'

As they were together 24/7, the band admit that there were times when they all needed to have some time to themselves to relax. As Jon says, 'We all got on brilliantly. In fact, I don't think we'd ever got on better, which was great because I was worried that it could go the other way. But there are times when you need your own space, so we would find a quiet corner of the bus and have a think or whatever. I think it kept us sane through the madness.'

Backstage Escapades

Forget diva-like dressing-room demands, all the S Clubbers wanted was water, fruit and plenty of towels at their disposal.

'Oh, and I wanted blue M&M's. But only the blue ones so someone had to spend ages picking them all out!' Hannah jokes.

M&M's aside, the band had to make sure that they were eating well at all times. Hours of dancing non-stop onstage every night meant they had to keep their energy levels up. But thanks to tour catering, they feasted on steaks, chicken, pasta, Sunday roasts and just about anything else they could get their hands on!

RU up 4 it, Brad?

Jo's ready to go

Paul's eyes definitely have it

No last-minute nerves for Jon

Wasssuppp!

Hannah also had to stock up on energy drinks and salt tablets to keep her going.

'I'm not very good at drinking enough water and I sweat loads onstage, so the salt tablets helped me, while the energy drinks really kept me going,' she explains.

Hair down or up, Rach?

Tina joins the 'Braidy' bunch

The backstage area is where competition winners get to do 'meet-and-greets' with the band, which is something that means a lot to the S Club crew.

'Being on tour gives us the opportunity to meet loads of fans, which is lovely,' says Bradley, as the others nod in agreement.

Necks, please?

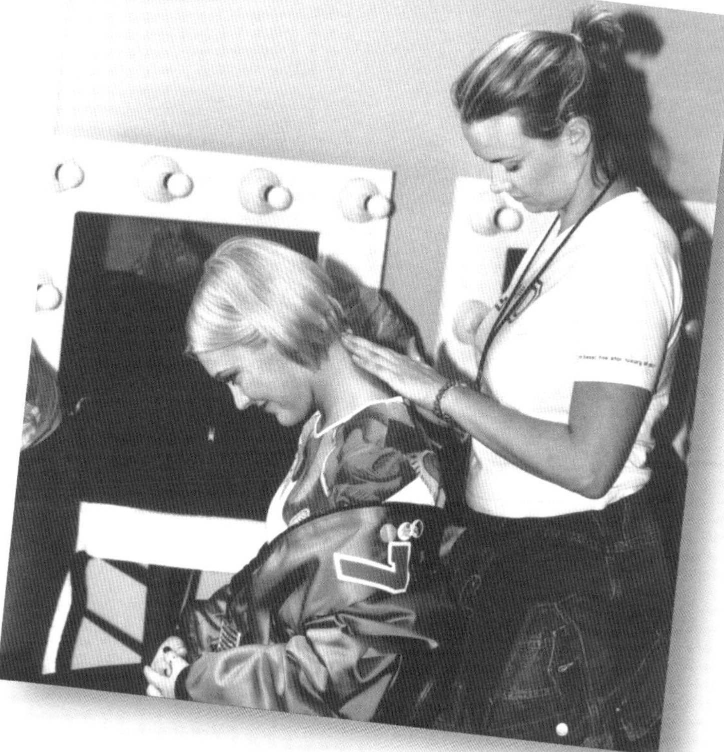

'At some venues we had about 170 people coming backstage, which was pretty hectic, but it gave us a great opportunity to chat to a lot of the fans. And because they were so excited about being there, it got us more excited about performing.'

And there were certainly some bonkers goings-on backstage. At one venue, Jon and Hannah created their very own 'beach' in their dressing room.

Hannah explains why: 'We were in Dublin and it was a lovely sunny day. We had a few hours off and Jon and I had spotted this river when we were travelling to the venue, so we decided to pack a picnic and go down there. But then we got called back to do some work and we were really disappointed, so we decided to create our own beach! We used some material that we found in our dressing room to make the sea and we had our picnic in there. Whenever people walked in we'd make them take their shoes and socks off so that they could paddle in the sea. People thought we'd gone completely mad!'

Well, they do say life's a beach ...

Just chillin' for a moment

Tina gets lippy

Time for a last-minute touch-up

Listen up, everyone!

You talkin' 'bout me?

When it came to getting ready to hit the stage, the band would all do a stretching routine to prepare them for their energetic dance routines, and then gather together for a vocal warm-up.

Jo admits that she really needed peace and quiet before a show and would often lock herself in her dressing room if she was feeling nervous.

'I sometimes needed some time by myself just to get prepared. I did get nervous quite a lot and that was the only thing that would keep me calm.'

Can you hear me at the back, guys?

Rachel makes her entrance. Wow!

'We didn't have any kind of dramatic way of psyching ourselves up for the shows,' Jon reveals. 'We did have a group hug on the first night, but that was about it. I think most of the time things didn't need to be said. All it would be is a smile and a nod to each other right before we went onstage, and that would be enough.'

Pants!

The S Club tour was relatively disaster free, apart from one huge headache in Dublin, as Paul explains.

'Someone dropped a two-litre bottle of water all over the engineering desk meaning that we either had to go on and mime the whole show – which none of us wanted to do – or the gig was going to have to be cancelled. We were all gutted, but we felt quite rock 'n' roll at the same time.'

Thankfully, in the end, some good old-fashioned hair dryers saved the day and the band managed to go on with the show.

The only other near-catastrophe involved Tina's knickers. Luckily, someone saved the day just in the, er, nick of time. Kindly explain all, Tina!

'Well, they weren't actually proper knickers. They were like these granny shorts that I had to wear over my proper knickers, underneath my ballet dress because the split was really high. Only, this one night I left them in my hotel room and I was panicking about going onstage without them.

'Luckily, someone rushed back to the hotel and got them for me just before I had to do my ballet. Oh dear. I can't actually believe that I've just told you that story!'

Ain't No Party

Well, actually, there were loads! The seven had plenty of cracking parties on tour, and even when there wasn't an 'official' do happening, they would all gather together in someone's hotel room to have fun and wind down after the gigs.

'If there was nothing going on and we didn't feel like going out we'd just go to someone's room and sit around and chat and have a laugh. It was a good way of relaxing,' says Rachel, 'but we also went to some really good clubs and stuff.'

They celebrated overcoming their near disaster in Dublin by going to a bar called Lillie's Bordello – a hot favourite with other bands like Westlife, Five and U2 – until four in the morning. It was a night that Bradley remembers well.

'We all partied together – all of the crew, the dancers and the support bands. We went out and we laughed until we cried. Some other nights were pretty mad as well. But it can be difficult for us to party sometimes because if we go to a bar or club we literally get everyone in there queuing up to meet us and shake our hands. So sometimes we'd spend the entire night shaking people's hands and we didn't really get a chance to party. But it's all good.'

Everyone agrees that Jon was the biggest party animal on the tour, with Bradley a close second.

'I think me and Bradley share the party-animal title equally,' Jon insists. 'We got really close on that tour because most nights, when the show was finished, we'd go out to clubs and bars with loads of other people. There was always a big group wherever we went, and Bradley and I were always a part of it.'

Everyone was out in force when it came to the 'wrap' party on the last night of the tour, and they were certainly in the mood to let their hair down and dance the night away.

'We went to this great bar in Birmingham and danced all night,' says Tina, with a smile. 'It was brilliant because a lot of our friends and family came along so we got a chance to catch up. It was definitely a night to remember.'

This Is My Moment

Everyone who saw the show agreed it was nothing short of incredible. But what did the band members enjoy most about their terrific tour?

Hannah

Favourite tracks to perform

‘“S Club Party”, “Bring the House Down” and “Bring It All Back”. They funked up “Bring It All Back” and changed the backing beat so it sounded brilliant. It was an extended mix and the boys did a really good dance break in it, which got a great reaction from the audience. I also loved doing the head banging in “S Club Party”. The older people in the audience really got into that!’

Best memory

‘I loved my entrance when I came down from the top of the stage. Thankfully, I wasn’t scared because it wasn’t that high and I’m not afraid of heights anyway, so I just really enjoyed it.’

Jon

Favourite tracks to perform

'I thought "Bring the House Down" and "S Club Party" were wicked.'

Best memory

'The whole thing. It was just the best experience and I miss it so much. I would love to be there now. It's always been my dream to stand on the Wembley stage and shout 'Hello, Wembley!', and I got to do it. It was an amazing moment. I also loved doing my solo track, which was a cover of Michael Jackson's "She's Out of My Life". It's the same song that I performed at the S Club 7 auditions, so it's always been a lucky song for me. I thought it would be cool to do it on tour and it was. I loved it.'

Paul

Favourite tracks to perform

'I thought the live version of "Two in a Million" was really good because it was a bit different.'

Best memory

'There are so many that I can't remember any particular ones. I think just getting onstage every night and feeling the buzz from the audience is something that I'll never forget. I also think it was great that our fans got to see a different side to us with us rocking out and stuff. That was pretty cool.'

Rachel

Favourite tracks to perform

'I loved "S Club Party" because we were in the biker stuff, and it was wicked when we came out in our rock gear in "Bring the House Down".'

Best memory

'There were great bits about the whole show for me. I absolutely loved it when they showed the footage of what we'd done over the past few years. That was lovely. The tour was definitely the highlight of my career so far. It was a chance to get out there and sing live to the fans and show what we could do. It made me feel so proud looking out into the crowd and seeing everyone singing along.'

Jo

Favourite tracks to perform

'I loved doing "S Club Party" in the rock outfits because I don't think anyone expected us to do it. And I loved doing "Never Had a Dream Come True" in our white suits.'

Best memory

'Every night before the show they used to flash up pictures of different bands and celebrities on the video wall. Every time they flashed up a picture of us the crowd would go wild and I just loved that. What a feeling!'

Bradley

Favourite tracks to perform

'Definitely "S Club Party" and "Bring It All Back". And I've got to say "Friday Night", not just because I sing it, but because every night I'd try something new with my voice and I got really into it.'

Best memory

'I just loved the fact that we got to sing live because we can all sing our hearts out. I think that was the biggest buzz for us all – getting out there each night and seeing how things got better and better as the tour went on.'

Tina

Favourite tracks to perform

'There wasn't one that I didn't enjoy. But I think all of us really enjoyed "S Club Party" because we got to do something a little bit different and show a different side to us.'

Best memory

'The whole tour was one big highlight for me. It was like a breath of fresh air. I really enjoyed getting to do my ballet every night because it's a big part of my background, and it was nice to show something new to the fans.'

That's Not All, Folks!

If you missed out on the tour last time round, or you did get to see it and are desperate for more, never fear! S Club will be hitting the tour trail again in February 2002, and here's a bit of insider info on what you can expect.

'It's basically going to be bigger and more colourful, with more new songs,' reveals Hannah. 'We'll still be performing the old favourites, but we'll also be performing tracks from our third album. We're going to keep the same band and dancers because we had such a great time with them on the last tour, and I think all of us are desperate to get back out there.'

'I can't wait,' says Paul with a grin. 'I think we all had an even better time than we expected on the first tour, and we're going to work really hard to make sure this one is even bigger and better.'

Don't Stop the Music

A new single, a new album and some hot favourites. It's time to talk music.

Which is your favourite out of all your singles?

'Don't Stop Movin''. It broke new ground for us. It's funky and everyone genuinely likes it. I turn it up if I hear it on the radio because the tune is phat.'

Bradley

'Reach' because it's a happy song and always puts a smile on my face. And it always makes me laugh when Paul comes out in the middle of the song and does his Elvis legs. I also love 'Never Had a Dream Come True' and 'Have You Ever'.

Jo

'Don't Stop Movin''. I think it was a really different sound to what was out there when we released it. It had an eighties' feel to it and was really funky.

Tina

'Don't Stop Movin''. I loved it the first time I heard it, and even now whenever it comes on anywhere I have to dance. I can't help it. If someone else had released it I would definitely have bought it.'

Jon

'Don't Stop Movin''. I think it's our best song by a mile.'

Paul

I've got four: 'Don't Stop Movin'', 'Never Had a Dream Come True', 'Natural' and our new single 'Have You Ever'.

Rachel

'Don't Stop Movin''. It always makes me want to dance.'

Hannah

What kind of music do you listen to in your spare time?

"Michael Jackson, Dire Straits, Daft Punk, Train, Travis, Red Hot Chili Peppers, Faithless and Destiny's Child."

Hannah

"I haven't got one style of music that I listen to these days. I listen to a lot of Motown stuff, and I still love Madonna and Michael Jackson."

Rachel

"I listen to so many different types of music. I'll listen to a lot of Motown, but then I'll also listen to Limp Bizkit, Busta Rhymes, Moby and Travis. And I love listening to lovely voices like The Carpenters or Eva Cassidy."

Jo

"I listen to rock, but I'm not that keen on all the American Nu-metal stuff that's big at the moment."

Paul

"I listen to a lot of garage and R'n'B, but I'm not blind to what's going on in the charts. I always keep an eye on them."

Bradley

"I listen to a lot of R'n'B. I tend to like stuff that's a bit harder than pop, but I also like some pop as well."

Tina

"I love old Motown music and En Vogue, Lionel Ritchie and Stevie Wonder. And I also love stuff like Lucy Pearl, Tori Amos, Missy Elliott and Alanis Morissette. A real range."

Jon

'Have You Ever'

S Club's new single is a beautiful ballad called 'Have You Ever', which all the band love, and rate as one of their top tracks.

'It's got a definite R'n'B and soul flavour to it. It's really cool.' says Bradley.

All the royalties from the sales of the single will go to this year's Children in Need appeal – something which the band are overjoyed about. As Rachel says, 'It means so much to us because it's such a great cause. That's definitely one of the great perks about being in the band – being able to help in some way. It's great to be involved and it means a lot to us.'

Jon continues, 'It's a really lovely track. There are going to be two versions of it. One with just us on it, and another which is going to have lots of British school kids singing on it. It will be really nice for them to be able to get involved as well.'

It's not the first time that S Club 7 have done their bit for Children in Need. They also donated the proceeds from their past single 'Never Had a Dream Come True' to the charity.

'I hope we make even more money than before because that's what it's all about. We all feel very privileged to be able to help,' says Jo, with a smile.

The All-new Album

November sees the release of S Club's third album, *Sunshine*, and all the gang agree that it's their best album yet.

Hannah explains why: 'It's really diverse, like our first two albums, but it's a little bit more grown-up. It's much more us, because as well as having the fun tracks on it, it's got some cooler, more laid-back tracks.'

'There are some really cool songs on there. I couldn't pick a favourite because I genuinely like them all,' says Tina, smiling.

Rachel agrees. 'I'm really, really proud of this album because I think it's the best one that we've done so far. There isn't one song that I don't like. And a lot that I love.'

'I really like the track "Summertime Feeling", and also "Stronger", which is like a housey dance tune,' adds Paul. 'I think people will see a real difference with this album, but there's still a lot of fun, poppy stuff on there.'

Jo already has a favourite track. 'Rachel does this song called "Show Me Your Colours", which I think is great. It's kind of guitar-based and is just a brilliant song.'

'I'm really pleased because I got to write a couple of songs on the album,' says Bradley, looking incredibly happy. 'I wrote a track called "Right Guy", which is also on the B-side of the "Don't Stop Movin'" single. It's got a real eighties' vibe to it and I also co-produced it. It's cool because writing and producing is something that I've always wanted to get involved in. This album is really exciting because I think it's going to surprise a lot of people, but I also think the fans will love it.'

S-creen Club 7

As if being one of the biggest pop bands in the world wasn't enough, S Club 7 also have three hugely successful TV series under their superstar belts.

The first two series, *Miami 7* and *LA 7*, have been watched by over ninety-million people in over 100 countries, and the new series, *Hollywood 7*, has been proving just as popular.

But who was it that couldn't stop fluffing their lines during its filming? Discover all, as S Club talk TV!

Hooray for Hollywood

The first thing Hannah remembers when she looks back on filming *Hollywood 7* are the early mornings!

'There was a lot to get done in a short amount of time, so we were up at the crack of dawn every day,' she says, doing a comedy yawn.

'The schedules are always really tight so it's quite intense while we're filming,' Paul chips in, 'and we get told off for messing around sometimes because everyone around us is panicking about getting it done. We're usually a bit more laid-back about it, while the director and everyone gets really stressed.'

And it seems as though Jo was usually the one getting into trouble: 'I always get the giggles and get told off, which just makes me laugh even more. I always try and warn the director at the start of filming that I'm like that, and I warn them not to tell me off because they'll just end up getting more annoyed. But do they listen?'

'It's bad, because there are some days where we can't stop laughing, no matter how hard we try,' Jon says, 'but this series was really good to film because we did loads of location work all over LA. I know the place inside out now because we went to different places practically every day. And we got to work with a lot of the same crew and production team that we've worked with on the other series, so that was cool.'

'It's always fun filming the shows. It's a real adventure and *Hollywood 7* was no different,' adds Rachel. 'You can't not enjoy doing it. Music is my first love and I get more of a buzz out of performing onstage than acting in the series, but I still have a great time, and getting to act is a real bonus.'

Tina says that *Hollywood 7* was her favourite series to film out of the three they've done so far. 'I think I was probably just more comfortable with the acting because I knew what I was doing more. It was as if I dropped my shoulders about five inches and started really enjoying myself.'

The seven may have had fun, but filming wasn't without its

embarrassing moments. Hannah's face went a fetching shade of scarlet when they had to sing a new track called 'You' on LA's trendy Venice Beach in front of hundreds of passers-by.

'We had to sing it while we were hanging out at this magazine stand, looking at photos of ourselves. People were looking at us as if we were from another planet,' she says, blushing at the memory.

'And it was also embarrassing when I had this scene when I got knocked out by a girl during an argument,' says Jon, smiling. 'I must have looked sooooo stupid.'

So who was most guilty of fluffing their lines during the filming of *Hollywood 7*?

'I think we all were at some point,' says Bradley, grinning. 'I could be really bad sometimes. I had this line that went, "Why can't I have a higher-profile romance?". I had to say it over and over again because I kept tripping over the words. And then Jon had to say it, and he couldn't get it right either. We had to do so many different takes. Things like that can drive you mad!'

Home Is Where the Heart Is

There isn't one band member who doesn't enjoy the acting side of S Club 7. (Bradley especially liked getting to kiss a gorgeous twenty-five-year-old girl in their TV special *Back to the 50's*), although a few of them do find themselves getting homesick when they're working so far away from home for long periods of time.

Jo, in particular, misses her boyfriend and her two dogs. 'I live a really quiet family life, with my boyfriend, Lee, and our dogs when I'm at home. I've got a bichon

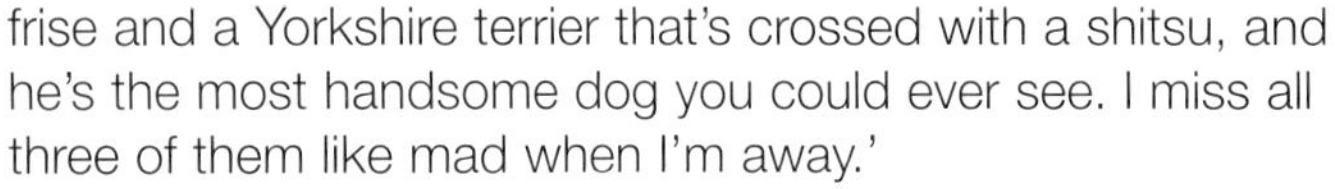

frise and a Yorkshire terrier that's crossed with a shitsu, and he's the most handsome dog you could ever see. I miss all three of them like mad when I'm away.'

Rachel misses London full stop, and reckons she could never base herself in LA full time.

'I'm a real London girl at heart. Although I really like LA, I couldn't leave London to live anywhere else. It's my home.'

Paul shares her feelings. 'I really like LA, which is why I preferred filming *LA 7* and *Hollywood 7* to *Miami 7*. But I couldn't live there full time because I can get homesick just being there for a few months.'

'I think being away from home for the first series, *Miami 7*, really changed me,' Bradley admits. 'I made some good friends, but I still spent quite a lot of time on my own. I did a lot of thinking and starting seeing things differently. Maybe it was because I was missing my friends and family, but it definitely made me wake up to a few things and put a different perspective on life, so in that way it was a really positive thing.'

Is the Film for Reel?

You've probably heard loads of rumours about there being an

S Club 7 film in the pipeline, and the brilliant news is that the rumours are 100% true.

'I can't reveal too much,' says Rachel excitedly, 'but it's going to be very, very funny and will be really different to all the TV series. We've all got some great ideas and there's a fantastic storyline to it. But that's all I'm saying.'

The others are equally tight-lipped about their new project.

'There are loads of ideas flying around at the moment and it all sounds excellent, but we're keeping quiet about it because we want it to be a surprise for everyone,' is all Paul will say.

Because the film is going to be a comedy, the group would love to get a great British comedian in on the act. The bands' top choices include Richard Blackwood, Kathy Burke, Harry Enfield, Lily Savage, Lee Evans and Graham Norton. But who knows who will pop up?

Reach For the Future

If you think S Club 7 have already packed a lot into their incredible three years together, you can rest assured that there's a whole lot more to come. As well as the new album, tour and film, there are definitely more smash hit singles on the way.

Fasten your seat belts, S Club fans, the only way is up ...

WWW.SCLUB.COM